Vasco da Gama

and the Portuguese Explorers

Explorers of New Worlds

Daniel Boone and the Exploration of the Frontier
Christopher Columbus and the Discovery of the New World
Francisco Coronado and the Exploration of the American Southwest
Hernando Cortés and the Conquest of Mexico
Lewis and Clark: Explorers of the Louisiana Purchase
Vasco da Gama and the Portuguese Explorers
Ferdinand Magellan and the First Voyage Around the World
Marco Polo and the Wonders of the East
Juan Ponce de León and the Search for the Fountain of Youth
Hernando de Soto and the Exploration of Florida

Vasco da Gama

and the Portuguese Explorers

Jim Gallagher

Chelsea House Publishers
Philadelphia

Prepared for Chelsea House Publishers by:
OTTN Publishing, Warminster, PA

CHELSEA HOUSE PUBLISHERS
Editor in Chief: Stephen Reginald
Managing Editor: James D. Gallagher
Production Manager: Pamela Loos
Art Director: Sara Davis
Director of Photography: Judy L. Hasday
Senior Production Editor: LeeAnne Gelletly
Series Designer: Keith Trego

First Printing
1 3 5 7 9 8 6 4 2

Library of Congress Cataloging-in-Publication Data

Gallagher, Jim, 1969–
    Vasco da Gama and the Portuguese explorers / by Jim
    Gallagher.
p.   cm. – (Explorers of new worlds)
Includes bibliographical references and index.
Summary: Discusses the travels of Vasco da Gama and
other Portuguese explorers who helped establish an
extensive empire for their country.
ISBN 0-7910-5514-0 (hc)
1. Gama, Vasco da, 1469–1524 Journeys Juvenile litera-
ture. 2. Explorers–Portugal–Biography Juvenile litera-
ture. 3. Discoveries in geography–Portugal Juvenile lit-
erature. [1. Gama, Vasco da, 1469–1524. 2. Explorers. 3.
Portugal–History–Period of discoveries, 1385–1580.] I.
Title. II. Series.
G285.G35   1999
910'.92–dc21   99-22258
[B]   CIP

Contents

I	Setting Sail	7
2	A Nation of Seafarers	11
3	Along the Coast of Africa	21
4	Around the Cape of Good Hope	31
5	The Voyage of Vasco da Gama	41
6	The Riches of the Indies	49
	Chronology	58
	Glossary	60
	Further Reading	62
	Index	63

Vasco da Gama was not an experienced sailor. However, Portugal's king had groomed him to lead an sailing expedition around the tip of Africa. Gama's goal was to establish a trade route to India.

Setting Sail I

A t dawn on the morning of July 8, 1497, nearly 200 sailors, each carrying a lighted candle, walked slowly through the streets of Lisbon, Portugal. The group was followed by townspeople. When the men reached Lisbon's large harbor, they paused. A Catholic priest gave a blessing, and asked God to forgive the sins of "those who might perish in this discovery or conquest."

Then King Manoel I of Portugal spoke. The crowd was silent as he made a solemn promise to God. If the mission was successful, he would build a large new cathedral in Lisbon that would contain the tombs of Portugal's kings.

When the king had finished speaking, small boats took the sailors to the larger ships they would take on their voyage of discovery. The ships were going to sail around Africa into unknown waters, in hopes of becoming the first Europeans to reach the mysterious lands of India and Asia by sea.

As the sailors boarded the four ships, which were a type called *caravels*, and prepared to set sail, a brown-haired, bearded man began issuing orders. His name was Vasco da Gama. A Portuguese noble-man, Gama had been selected to lead the expedition. He was a strong leader, smart and persistent.

His four caravels were not very large, but they were well-built. A Portuguese hero named Bartolomeu Dias had designed the two biggest, the *São Gabriel* and the *São Rafael*. The ships had wide, rounded hulls. This would allow them to sail close to the African coast without scraping bottom.

Nine years earlier, Dias had proved that it was possible to sail around the southern tip of Africa. Now, Gama would try to build on the discoveries of Dias and other courageous Portuguese mariners. He and his men did not know what they would find once they passed the farthest point reached by Dias in 1488. Perhaps they would encounter people who would be hostile. Maybe the route to Asia would be blocked by an unexpected land mass. Some of the uneducated, superstitious sailors even feared they would find sea monsters.

The Portuguese had been preparing for this mission for nearly two years. Vasco da Gama had the best maps and tools for **navigation** that were available in the late 15th century. The crews of his four ships were experienced sailors, and the caravels were stocked with enough food for three years. They were armed with 20 **bombards**, a type of cannon that hurled large stone balls. Stone markers carved with the royal crest of Portugal were stored in each ship's hold. Gama would place these markers in new lands to claim them for King Manoel.

One of the sailors on the *São Rafael* kept a personal log of the journey. Passages from the journal, later published as a book called *The Roteiro*, show the anxious feelings that most members of the crew were probably feeling as the four Portuguese ships sailed away from their safe harbor in Lisbon. "May God our Lord permit us to accomplish this voyage in his service," the unknown sailor wrote.

This 15th-century artwork shows a caravel, the popular sailing vessel developed by the Portuguese. A caravel had a broad hulls and a high and narrow deck at the at the back. The sturdy ship was very popular among explorers.

A Nation of Seafarers

2

Portugal is a small country located on the Iberian Peninsula. It borders the Atlantic Ocean. At the start of the 15th century, Portugal was a poor kingdom. Within 100 years, however, Portugal would be one of the richest and most powerful nations in Europe.

Before the country of Portugal was established, two strong kingdoms ruled the peninsula during the Middle Ages. (Eventually, these two kingdoms, Aragon and Castille, would merge to form Spain.) At this time, most of the inhabitants of the Iberian Peninsula were Christian.

Around the year 750 A.D., the people living on the

peninsula became involved in a religious war. A tribe from northern Africa called the **Moors** invaded the Iberian Peninsula. The Moors were **Muslims**, which means they followed a religion called Islam. Because Christians and Muslims hated each other, centuries of bloody fighting resulted.

In 1179, a Christian leader forced the Moors away from an area of the Atlantic coast. He created the kingdom of Portugal, and crowned himself King Afonso I. However, war between the Christians and the Moors would continue for nearly 300 years.

By the year 1400, Portugal's population was about one million. Two factors would help make this small nation become one of the most powerful in Europe. The first was that Portugal developed one of Europe's largest fishing fleets. Portuguese sailors became very skilled at navigation, and craftsmen learned how to build seaworthy sailing ships. These would be necessary for long journeys. The second factor was that people became interested in finding new lands—and the riches they might contain.

Europeans became interested in exploration with the discovery of long-lost books on **geography** that had been written by the ancient Greeks and Romans. A more modern book, written by Marco

Polo in 1297, also captured peoples' attention.

As a young man, Marco Polo had visited Asia by journeying overland. He spent 25 years traveling through the Far East. When Marco returned home, he brought many items that were not available in Europe. These included ivory and jade jewelry, fine silk cloth, and perfume. He also brought *spices*, such as pepper, nutmeg, mace, cinnamon, and cloves. These could be used to preserve meat or to improve the taste of food. Other items, such as sugar, coffee, and tea, were also called spices. Europeans wanted these exotic spices, so traders were soon following Marco Polo's route to the East.

In the century after Marco Polo's death, the trip became increasingly dangerous. The Mongol Empire, which had protected the traveling merchants, was growing weaker. With strong armies, the Ottoman Turks took over control of the Middle East and western Asia. The Turks were Muslims, and therefore were enemies of the European Christians. They attacked traders who were trying to reach China through their lands.

People still wanted spices, so new trade routes developed. Muslim traders purchased silk, spices, and other goods in Asia. The goods were shipped to ports in India or the Middle East, then transported by **caravans** to a pair of Italian cities on the eastern Mediterranean Sea, Venice and Genoa. From there, the goods were distributed throughout Europe.

The spice trade soon made Venice and Genoa the wealthiest cities in Europe. Monarchs of other countries were jealous of their riches. These kings wished they could buy the spices directly from Asia. This would eliminate the fees charged by the Muslim middlemen and the merchants of Venice and Genoa. Land routes to Asia were too dangerous, so the monarchs started looking to the sea.

Portugal was ideally suited to find a sea route to Asia. It had become a nation of seafarers, with a strong navy and a sailing tradition. And in the 1400s, a member of Portugal's royal family would set in motion events that within 100 years would make his country very wealthy and powerful. His name was Prince Henry the Navigator.

Prince Henry was the third child of King João of Portugal. He knew that he would probably never become king. His older brother, Duarte, would become king when João died. If something happened to Duarte, Henry's brother Pedro would rule until Duarte's son was old enough to assume the

Marco Polo's stories of the Far East inspired trader caravans, such as this one shown on an old map, to travel to Asia and bring spices back to Europe.

crown. Because Henry didn't have to worry about ruling the country, he turned his attention to subjects that interested him: religion and exploration.

In 1410, King João decided to attack Ceuta, an important Muslim-held port on the coast of north Africa. After gathering information for several years, João and his generals decided the city was vulnerable to an attack from the sea. They began to plan the assault. Henry and his brothers were placed in charge of the attack. Henry's job was to assemble the fleet.

When the 200-ship Portugese fleet arrived in Ceuta's harbor on August 15, 1414, the Muslims were totally surprised. The Portugese captured the city in a day. Prince Henry and his brothers were all involved in the hand-to-hand fighting.

The victory inspired Henry in two ways. While building the fleet he had come into contact with many experienced sailors. From them, he learned how a well-supplied ship could stay at sea for a long time. Also, the victory proved how sea power could defeat the Muslims. Henry was deeply religious, and wanted to continue fighting to spread Christianity. Portugal was too small to wage a serious war against the powerful Ottoman Empire, though, and the other countries of Europe were no longer interested in religious *crusades*.

During the next few years, Henry served in the

> **To keep Ceuta's spies from suspecting an attack, King João pretended to be angry with Holland. (Secretly, João told the Dutch ruler about his plan to attack the Moslem stronghold and the duke, a fellow Christian, approved.) The Moors believed the Portuguese were preparing for a war with Holland until Henry's fleet appeared on the horizon.**

Prince Henry the Navigator (1394–1460) is one of the most important figures of Portuguese history. The school of navigation that he founded and the missions of exploration that he encouraged helped Portugal become a rich and powerful nation in the 16th century.

military. In 1418, Ceuta was attacked by an army of Moors. Henry led a Portuguese army that fought off the attack. Then he spent three months in Ceuta. While there, he heard many stories about a rich land that was 20 days journey to the south. The Muslim traders of Ceuta traveled across a vast desert until they reached a forested and fertile country. There, they traded with the native people, bringing back ivory, gold, spices, and other goods. The Europeans called this country Guinea.

When Prince Henry returned to Portugal, he decided to seek a sea route to Guinea. The prince was not yet thinking about sailing around Africa or trying to find the rich lands of Asia to the East. He merely thought a Portuguese trade route to Guinea could be very rewarding. Of course, the prince also wanted to probe the Muslims' strength in Africa. If the empire was weak at the fringes, perhaps it could be destroyed by the Christian nations of Europe.

Henry moved to a small village called Sagres in 1419. It was on a high cliff that overlooked the Atlantic Ocean. He invited sailors, sea captains, geographers, mapmakers, travelers, and scholars to visit him and share their knowledge and ideas. A shipbuilding industry was established nearby. Eventually, the sturdy ships called caravels would be developed at Sagres. These ships soon became the most popular vessels used by oceangoing explorers.

In 1420, Henry sent his first sailing expedition south. When a storm blew the ship off course to the west, it landed on an island in the Atlantic. The island was one of many that became known as the Madeira Islands. When Henry heard the news, he sent Portugese settlers to colonize the Madeiras.

Over the next few years, Henry sent ships west to find islands in the Atlantic. They visited the Canary Islands and discovered a new group: the

Azores. Settlements on these islands would become bases for future explorers. Other ships were sent south to explore the coast of Africa. However, the sailors were afraid to sail beyond a rocky *cape* on the mainland just south of the Canary Islands. (A cape is a point of land that projects into the sea.)

Between 1422 and 1434, Prince Henry sent at least 14 missions to pass this point, Cape Bojador. All were unsuccessful. The sailors feared the unknown waters, called the "Sea of Darkness," that lay beyond Cape Bojador. There were stories of great fogs and tricky currents. Some felt that once past the cape, a ship could never sail back. Farther south, it was rumored, the sea boiled and the sun burned men's skin black. No man had ever sailed around Cape Bojador and lived to tell the tale.

Finally, a captain named Gil Eanes passed Cape Bojador in 1434. When he returned to Sagres, he told Prince Henry that the Sea of Darkness "was as easy to sail as the waters at home." The first major hurdle to exploring the coast of Africa had been passed.

Along the Coast
of Africa

The coastline of Sagres, where Prince Henry's 15th-century school of navigation was based. This was a familiar sight to Portuguese sailors departing on missions to explore the coast of Africa.

A year after Gil Eanes's ships rounded Cape Bojador, Prince Henry sent Eanes on another mission. Another young captain, Afonso Baldaia, went with him. They landed on a sandy beach 200 miles past Bojador. There, they found the footprints of men and camels. This proved that men lived in the southern regions of Africa. In 1436, Baldaia sailed alone down the coast of Africa. He landed 100 miles farther down the coast, at the mouth of an inlet that he called Rio de Oro–the River of Gold. When Baldaia returned, he brought back a valuable cargo of sealskins. His men also reported seeing 19 natives armed with spears.

However, after this mission Prince Henry's voyages of exploration stopped for six years. Henry's brother, Duarte, had become king of Portugal a few years earlier. He was planning to attack a strong Moorish city, Tangier. Henry was appointed one of the commanders. However, the Portuguese attack, in August 1437, failed miserably. Prince Henry's younger brother, Fernando, was captured by the Moors. He eventually died in prison.

King Duarte had been in poor health for several years. The capture and death of his youngest brother were hard on him as well. He died just over a year after the disastrous battle, in September 1438. With the king dead, a dispute arose over who would rule the kingdom. His son, Afonso, was still a child. A temporary ruler, called a *regent*, had to be chosen to lead the country until Afonso was old enough to take over. A *civil war* nearly broke out between supporters of Duarte's brother, Pedro, and those who wanted Duarte's wife to be Portugal's regent. For the next several years, Prince Henry tried to

help settle the crisis. He could not focus on exploration until 1441, when the situation was settled and
Pedro was named regent.

That year, Henry sent out two vessels. One was
commanded by Antão Gonçalves, the other by
Nuno Tristão. Tristão's ship was one of the newly
developed caravels. The two captains met south of
Rio de Oro. On a foray into the mainland, they captured 12 Africans. Gonçalves returned to Portugal
with the natives, but Tristão decided to keep exploring. He sailed to Cape Blanc, about 250 miles south
of Rio de Oro, before turning back.

The African natives interested the Portugese.
One of the natives, a chief named Adahu, taught
Henry a lot about Africa and the people who lived
there. As a good Christian, the prince wanted to
convert the Africans. As an explorer, he was interested in the information they could provide. But
others saw the the natives as a source of profit. They
could be captured and used as slaves.

In 1442, Gonçalves sailed back to Rio de Oro
with Adahu and two of the Africans. They
exchanged them for 10 slaves that Adahu's tribe had
captured and some gold dust. In 1443, Tristão sailed
100 miles past Cape Blanc. He landed at the island

of Arguim, captured 28 natives, and returned home. Eventually, the Portuguese established a trading station at Arguim—their first in tropical Africa.

The slave trade grew quickly. In 1444, over 200 natives were captured during an expedition to Arguim. They were brought to Portugal and sold at auction. These Africans were the first of millions who would be carried away chained in European ships over the next 400 years. By 1448, 25 Portugese trade caravels were visiting the African coast each year. Armed groups of sailors raided the interior for slaves. Others traded with local chiefs, who sold members of enemy tribes that they had captured.

Prince Henry's work was interrupted again in 1448 because of a civil war between the regent Pedro and King Afonso. Henry did not take part in the fighting. Although he was loyal to the king, he was sad when his brother Pedro was killed in battle in May 1449. After this trouble ended, another crisis began. The kingdom of Castille, which shared the Iberian Peninsula with Portugal, claimed that it, and not Portugal, should control the Canary Islands. Prince Henry's ships were needed for the war that broke out between Castille and Portugal. The fighting lasted nearly five years.

Portuguese captains exploring the coast of Africa started bringing natives back to Europe as slaves. Soon, the slave trade was an important source of revenue for Portugal.

In the mid-1450s, Portuguese sailors began exploring the African coast again. A seaman from Venice named Alvise Cadamosto entered Prince

During their years of discovery, the Portuguese
established many trading outposts along the western coast
of Africa. The remains of this small fort at Cape Verde is
a popular tourist spot today.

Henry's service in 1455. He was sent to visit the
colonies that Henry's captains had established, and
he found them to be thriving. Cadamosto sailed
south of Cape Blanc until he passed Cape Verde, the
westernmost point of Africa. From there, the continent begins to curve to the east. This made Henry
hope the passage around Africa might be near.

In 1456, Cadamosto discovered the Cape Verde Islands off the coast of Africa. That same year, a Portuguese navigator named Diogo Gomes led a mission along the Gambia River, 100 miles south of Cape Verde. He returned with a great deal of information about new caravan routes. He had also traded cloth and beads for 180 pounds of gold.

By the time these expeditions returned, Prince Henry was 70 years old. He was not in good health. In 1460 he died. He had never visited the African shores to which he had sent so many mariners.

The trade routes that Henry's sailors had established brought a great deal of money to Portugal. However, King Afonso did not want to continue spending money on voyages of exploration that might not eventually pay off. As a result, there was little new exploration during the next nine years.

In 1469, a merchant from Lisbon named Fernão Gomes came up with an interesting proposal for King Afonso. He asked the king to give him exclusive rights to all trading on the coast of Guinea for five years. In return, Gomes would pay an annual fee, and would explore 400 miles of new coastline a year. Afonso agreed. Portugal's exploration of the African coast could continue at no cost to the king.

Between 1469 and 1474, Gomes's mariners explored more than 2,000 miles of new coastline. It had taken Prince Henry's expeditions 40 years to travel the same distance. Gomes's first expedition sailed nearly 600 miles past Cape Verde. The new captain discovered that after Cape Palma, the land turned sharply to the east. He returned, believing that a passage around the continent lay ahead.

In 1473, a captain named Fernando Pó passed the Niger River and the Gulf of Guinea. When he returned, Pó gave Gomes some bad news. Past the gulf, the African coastline turned to the south again. In 1474, Lopo Gonçalves became the first European to direct his ship across the **equator**, the imaginary line that divides the northern and southern halves of the world, or **hemispheres**.

The missions organized by Fernão Gomes made him very wealthy. His captains brought back slaves, ivory, gold, and spices. As the Portuguese advanced along the African coast, they built forts, supply bases, and trading posts. These would serve as bases at which future voyages could stop for supplies before traveling further down the unexplored coast.

After five years, King Afonso decided not to extend Gomes's contract. Instead, he awarded the trade and exploration rights to his son, João. Like his great uncle Prince Henry, 19-year-old João was interested in geography and navigation.

However, he could not get started right away. From 1475 to 1479, Portugal and Castille were at war again. João served in the army. Then, when King Afonso died in 1481, the responsibility for governing Portugal fell on João's shoulders. When he was crowned King João II, he had to devote his attention to many issues.

But the king understood how important it was to keep seeking new lands. João gathered a group of smart advisors, who worked on maps and navigational tools. He also sent out a ship, commanded by Diogo Cão, on a

A picture of Prince João as a young boy. João later would become king of Portugal.

voyage of discovery. For Cão's voyage, King João ordered five-foot-tall marble pillars to be made. Called **padrãos**, each had a cross and the royal crest of Portugal carved into them. The king told Cão to place the pillars in prominent spots when he landed in new territory, to claim the land for Portugal.

Around the Cape of Good Hope

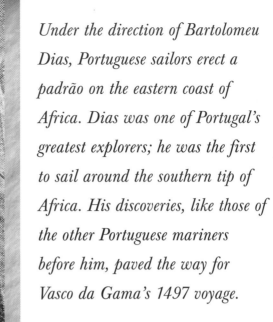

Under the direction of Bartolomeu Dias, Portuguese sailors erect a padrão on the eastern coast of Africa. Dias was one of Portugal's greatest explorers; he was the first to sail around the southern tip of Africa. His discoveries, like those of the other Portuguese mariners before him, paved the way for Vasco da Gama's 1497 voyage.

4

In May 1482, Diogo Cão set out from Lisbon to push the boundaries of African exploration. He soon passed the equator and Cape St. Catherine, the farthest point explored by the Portuguese at that time. From there, he sailed slowly south, following the African coastline.

It was a difficult trip. Cão's ship battled a strong current and unfavorable winds. The tropical heat drained the sailors' strength. Violent, frequent thunderstorms made navigation difficult. Also, the water was very shallow close to the coast. Cão's ship was designed to sail in the deep ocean. If he was not careful, rocks would rip out the bottom of his caravel. To keep from running aground, Cão often sailed 15 miles offshore. From this distance, he would examine the coast with a telescope.

As the expedition continued south, the crew's supply of drinking water grew lower and lower. Three times, Cão landed on the coast to look for fresh water. Each time, the captain was unsuccessful. Finally, he spotted a large, tree-lined bay. Cão directed his ship into the open water.

As the caravel sailed into the bay, he noticed a strong current rushing to the sea. He lowered a bucket into the brownish water and tasted it. The water was fresh, not salty. That meant it was coming from a river. Cão had discovered the mighty Congo River. It is the second-longest river in Africa, and fifth-longest in the world. The captain steered his vessel into the mouth of the river.

As the ship sailed slowly up the Congo, the sailors studied the thick jungle forest. They saw brightly colored birds, crocodiles lying on the riverbanks, and other odd animals. On a few occasions,

Natives steer a dugout canoe down the Congo River, one of the largest rivers in the world.

dark-skinned people stepped from the forest to watch the ship pass by. After traveling upstream for a few miles, the ship landed in a cove. Cão ordered one of King João's marble pillars to be erected.

The Congo River would make a good place to camp, Cão decided. His ships had been at sea for a long time. At the camp, his men could replenish the caravels' supplies of food and water. They could also make minor repairs to the ship and its sails.

The Portuguese remained in their camp for about a month. During that time, they became friendly with members of a local tribe, the Bakongo. The natives and Europeans learned to communicate with each other. The native leaders explained to Cão that they were ruled by a powerful king named Manikongo. His royal city, they told the captain, was far up the Congo River.

This news excited Cão. He sent a party of men upriver to search for the city. But Cão still had orders to explore the African coast. He decided to continue south, and made plans to pick up his men at the mouth of the Congo in a few months.

The caravel sailed another 500 miles down the coast of Africa. Cão named his stopping point Cape St. Mary, and placed a padrão there. He then returned to the Congo River. The party of explorers he had sent to find Manikongo had not yet returned. Cão decided to take some of the Bakongo hostage and return to Portugal. He could come back for the men later, but he wanted to report to King João.

When Diogo Cão returned to Lisbon in the spring of 1484, his story amazed the royal court. He had explored nearly 1,000 miles of new coastland. The four Africans he brought back with him did not become slaves. Instead, the King kept them in his palace and treated them like visiting royalty. João wanted them to tell Manikongo about his hospitality and kindness, and about Portugal's power and wealth, when Cão returned them to their homeland.

The next year, Diogo Cão set out from Lisbon again. This time, he took three ships. He was under orders not to return until he had rounded Africa.

On the way south, Cão stopped at the Congo River to drop off the four Bakongo tribesmen he had taken to Portugal. There was no sign of the men he had left to look for Manikongo. Cão decided to anchor his ships in the bay and wait for them. While the crews gathered food and fresh water, the captain took the smallest of his caravels to explore the river. Cão

Diogo Cão's voyage had a great impact on the world's future. King João had been considering a proposal for a westward voyage by an Italian navigator named Christopher Columbus. When Cão returned, the king turned Columbus down. Columbus, of course, later sailed west for Spain and discovered the New World.

went as far into Africa as he could. Eventually, a waterfall made it impossible to continue. The captain carved his name into the face of a large, rocky cliff, then returned to the mouth of the river.

No one knows exactly what happened next on Cão's 1485 voyage. He eventually left the camp and sailed south. He landed at a point 700 miles south of Cape St. Mary, and placed a padrão to claim the land for Portugal. He called the landing spot Cape Cross. Then the expedition returned to Lisbon. Some stories say that Diogo Cão died on the voyage. Others report that he lived, but that King João was angry and **banished** the brave captain because Cão did not continue all the way around Africa.

The king immediately began planning Portugal's next attempt. João decided to send two expeditions. The sea trip would be commanded by Bartolomeu Dias. An experienced sailor, Dias was given the same instructions as Diogo Cão: sail around Africa and find a route to the Indies. At the same time, two trusted men were sent to cross Africa by land. They were Pero da Covilhã and Afonso de Paiva. They set off on May 7, 1487.

A few months later, Dias was ready to set sail from Lisbon. He had three ships. Two were caravels.

Bartholomeu Dias bids farewell to the king and queen of Portugal. Dias commanded three ships on his voyage.

The third was a larger ship that he loaded with supplies, called a ***storeship***. It was not always easy to find food and water during a long journey. The storeship would allow Dias to stay at sea longer and therefore sail farther.

By the time Dias reached Cape Cross, high winds and tricky currents were making the voyage troublesome. Sailing the heavy storeship was especially difficult. Dias decided to leave it in a sheltered cove, and pressed on with his two caravels.

Within a few days, they sailed into a bad storm

that blew the ships off course. Dias and his men drifted far to the south and west, away from the coast. After 13 days, a west wind filled the sails, pushing the caravels back toward Africa. When Dias finally sighted land, he realized that his ships were sailing along the bottom of the continent.

The storm turned out to be lucky for Bartolomeu Dias. Without it, water currents would have made the trip very difficult. By swinging out into the South Atlantic, he had not only avoided the unfavorable currents, but picked up a strong west wind that helped him to quickly reach his destination.

On February 3, 1488, Dias landed on the east coast of Africa. He called the site Algoa Bay. After a short time, he pushed on to the mouth of the Great Fish River. There, he placed a padrão. He had reached the Indian Ocean. The riches of Asia lay to the north.

The captain wanted to try to find India, but his crew wanted him to turn back. The men were "weary, and terrified of the great seas through which they had pased," wrote a 16th-century Portuguese

Today, the spot where Dias first landed on the east coast of Africa is known as Mossel Bay.

historian named João de Barros. "[A]ll with one voice began to murmur, and demand that they proceed no farther."

Without the sailors' cooperation, Dias knew that he could not continue. Also, the ships were in poor shape, and the sails were ripped and frayed. Food was running low, and no one knew where it could be found on the east coast of Africa. Dias decided to turn back.

As the Portuguese sailed for home, the ships passed a high, rocky point jutting out into the sea. Dias had not noticed it earlier because of the storm that had blown his ships so far south of Africa. He named the point *Cabo Tormentoso*–the Cape of Storms. Dias made several stops on the journey back to Portugal. In the Gulf of Guinea, he rescued a shipwreck survivor, and he also picked up a load of gold dust. In December 1488, Dias and his men sailed into Lisbon's harbor.

Bartolomeu Dias's bold voyage had proved that the Portuguese could sail around Africa. All that was left was to sail north until the Indies were found. King João was so excited about the potential of this route that he renamed Cabo Tormentoso. He called it the Cape of Good Hope.

The Voyage of Vasco da Gama

5

Despite King João's excitement, he did not send out another voyage immediately. In fact, it would be nearly 10 years before Portuguese sailors sailed around the Cape of Good Hope again.

When Bartolomeu Dias returned, the king was still waiting to hear from his other explorers, Pero da Covilhã and Afonso de Paiva. When the two men had reached east Africa, they split up to learn as much as they could.

After Paiva died of a fever in 1490, Covilhã traveled to Abyssinia. First, he wrote a long letter to King João, reporting everything he had learned about harbors and ports. He also included information about the trade routes of the Indian Ocean.

Covilhã's letter reached King João in 1491. The king immediately began planning a voyage around Africa and through the Indian Ocean. But the plans were delayed by incredible news in the spring of 1493. A Spanish fleet commanded by Christopher Columbus had discovered the Indies by sailing west.

When Covilhã reached Abyssinia, he was received at the court of the emperor Alexander. The ruler liked his Portuguese visitor so much that he would not allow him to leave! Covilhã spent the next 30 years in Abyssinia.

Columbus's discovery set off a dispute between Spain and Portugal. King João felt that the route his sailors were developing—sailing along the coast of Africa then turning east and north to the Indies—was the best way to the East Indies. They feared competition from the Spanish, who thought Columbus had found the best way to Asia.

The Catholic Church had great power in Europe in the late 15th century. The rulers and most of the people of both Spain and Portugal were Catholic. The leaders explained the disagreement to the leader of the Catholic Church, Pope Alexander VI. In 1494, he settled the dispute by issuing the Treaty of Tordesillas. This agreement drew a line down the center of the Atlantic Ocean. The Pope gave Spain the right to explore and claim newly discovered lands to the west of the line. These included the islands found two years earlier by Columbus. (It was not until several years later that Europeans realized Columbus had discovered not the East Indies, but a new world–the Americas.) Portugal was given rights to the sea routes east of the line. This would allow the Portuguese to continue seeking the Indies by sailing around Africa.

In 1495, King João II died, and his son Manoel was crowned king. King Manoel ordered preparations for the voyage to the Indies to continue. He chose Vasco da Gama to command the expedition.

Not much is known about Vasco da Gama's early life. He was probably born around 1460, the year Prince Henry the Navigator died. His father was the governor of Sines, a fishing port in southern Portugal. Before being selected to lead the voyage to India, he had carried out some diplomatic missions for King João. These were probably intended to prepare him for the trip to the Indies.

Before the ships left Portugal, King Manoel ordered Gama to find the Indies and establish friendly relations with the countries that he reached. This would lead to a profitable trade with the East, the king hoped.

Gama would direct the fleet from his **flagship**, the *São Gabriel*. His older brother, Paulo da Gama, was captain of the *São Rafael*. The smallest of the ships was the *Berrio*. It was commanded by Nicolão Coelho, a knight who was related to King Manoel. The fourth vessel was a large ship that carried most of the supplies for the mission.

Many of the sailors had served with Bartolomeu Dias nine years earlier. Dias himself was aboard the *São Gabriel*. He had been appointed governor of a Portuguese colony that was on the route, so he would ride along for the first part of the voyage, providing information and advice.

A week after leaving Lisbon, Vasco da Gama's fleet passed the Canary Islands. On July 16, 1497, the ships anchored off Terra Alta. This was a spot on the coast with very high cliffs. It was often used as a landmark by the Portuguese sailors. They stayed for a day, fishing and relaxing, then sailed on. After leaving Terra Alta, Gama's ships sailed into a heavy

Vasco da Gama's three ships sail through the choppy waters of the South Atlantic. Gama followed Bartolomeu Dias's advice and swung his ships in an arc far to the west of the African coast, then back east.

fog. The caravels lost sight of each other, and became separated. Gama had anticipated this, and had given his captains instructions to regroup at the Cape Verde Islands.

The *Berrio* and the storeship were the first to arrive in the islands, followed by the *São Rafael* on July 22. When Vasco da Gama's ship did not appear, the other captains grew nervous. He finally showed up on July 26. The Portuguese were pleased to have their fleet together again, and they fired their bombards in welcome.

In the Cape Verde Islands, Bartolomeu Dias left the fleet to take his post as governor. The ships were restocked with food and fresh water. On August 3, Gama set off again.

The fleet sailed south along the coast of Africa for about 800 miles. Then Gama decided to change course. On his previous voyage nine years earlier, Dias had found that it was easier to sail away from the African coast, then let the western winds push the ships around it. This way, treacherous currents and bad weather could be avoided. The bad news was that this would make the trip longer, and that the Portuguese would be out of sight of land for a very long time.

Despite the protests of some members of the crew, the ships sailed in a wide arc to the southwest. At their farthest point west, Vasco da Gama's caravels were just about 600 miles off the undiscovered coast of South America. Then, when the captain thought he had sailed far enough, he ordered the ships to circle back to the southeast.

Week after week went by, with the ships still in the uncharted sea. There was no land where they could stop if there was trouble or they needed food. For more than three months, the four caravels pushed through the South Atlantic. The men began to suffer from a lack of vitamins, which causes a disease called *scurvy*. This disease appears when a person does not get enough fresh fruit and vegetables. Scurvy caused the sailors' gums to swell, and made the joints of their arms and legs hurt.

Finally, on November 4, 1497, one of Gama's men spotted the coast of Africa again. Three days later, the ships anchored at St. Helena Bay. They had spent 96 days away from the coast, and covered nearly 4,000 miles. This was the longest open-sea voyage ever made to that point. By comparison, Columbus's ships had been out of sight of land for only 33 days during his first voyage to the New World in 1492.

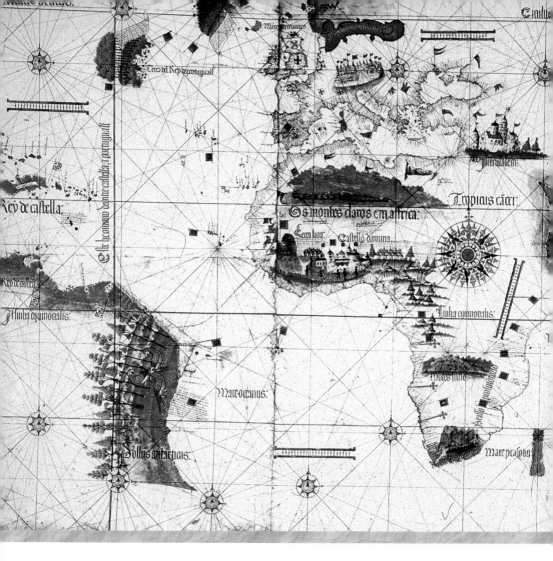

The Riches of
the Indies

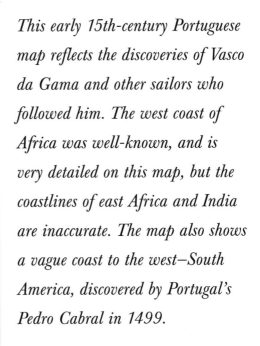

This early 15th-century Portuguese map reflects the discoveries of Vasco da Gama and other sailors who followed him. The west coast of Africa was well-known, and is very detailed on this map, but the coastlines of east Africa and India are inaccurate. The map also shows a vague coast to the west—South America, discovered by Portugal's Pedro Cabral in 1499.

6

asco da Gama's plan was not entirely successful. He was still on the west coast of Africa, about 100 miles before the Cape of Good Hope. The fleet stopped briefly so that the sailors could rest and repair their ships. They encountered some natives, who were friendly at first. Later, though, a party of sailors was attacked, and Gama and some others were wounded. The Portuguese decided to sail on.

After rounding the Cape of Good Hope, the caravels sailed into the Indian Ocean. After landing at Mossel Bay, the sailors divided the provisions and supplies from the storeship among the other three caravels. The storeship was then destroyed. Natives approached the sailors at Mossel Bay, but Gama thought they might attack. He fired his bombards and scared them away.

Before leaving Mossel Bay, the Portuguese placed a stone pillar and a wooden cross on the highest point. Then they set a northward course along the coast of Africa. On December 10, 1497, they passed a stone padrão at the Great Fish River. The marker showed where Dias had stopped–the farthest point of Portuguese exploration. Once Gama and his men passed it, they were in uncharted waters.

Because of strong, tricky ocean currents, the Portuguese made slow progress up the coast. By the time they reached the Quelimane River, sailors were sick with scurvy again and the ships needed repair. Gama decided to stop near the river. The fleet would stay there for more than a month.

After leaving Quelimane, the Portuguese stopped at Moçambique, a Muslim port several hundred miles farther up the coast. Gama and his men were excited at the riches available in the port city. However, the Muslims of Moçambique did not like or trust the Christian Portuguese. Because the uncharted waters were dangerous (the *Berrio* had been damaged when it hit a sand bar while entering the harbor), Gama offered to pay the local **sultan**, or ruler, for the use of two **pilots**. These were skilled sailors who knew the local waters. They could guide the Portuguese ships safely to the next port. The sultan agreed, but then tried to back out of the deal. He refused to let Gama have the pilots. Angry, the captain captured the pilots and bombed the town.

With very little help from their captives, the Portuguese eventually reached the port of Mombasa. There, the kidnapped pilots managed to escape. Gama captured two other Muslim sailors and forced them to guide him to the next port, Malindi. The sultan there was was friendly. He provided an experienced pilot who could guide Vasco da Gama to India. The ships left Malindi on April 24, 1498.

Less than a month later, on May 20, the Portuguese reached the city of Calicut, on the west coast of India. They were the first European vessels ever to reach India. At last, the long years of exploration that Prince Henry had started would pay off.

Vasco da Gama was fortunate that the sultan of Malindi was friendly. The ruler provided an experienced pilot to guide the Portuguese through the Indian Ocean.

When the caravels anchored, Gama sent a man into the city. He soon returned with someone who spoke Portuguese. "A lucky venture! A lucky venture," he told Gama. "Plenty of rubies, plenty of emeralds! You owe great thanks to God for having brought you to a country holding such riches!"

The Portuguese were amazed at the riches of Calicut. They saw gold jewelry and ornaments, pearls and precious stones, silks and bales of spices. However, Gama had brought cheap cloth and trinkets, not gold. These were fine for trading with the natives of Africa, but not for the sophisticated Arab and Indian traders of Calicut. The Portuguese would have to return home with just a small sample of the goods available for trade in India.

After spending the summer in Calicut, Gama decided to return home. The local ruler gave him a letter for King Manoel. It was written on a palm leaf. The letter read, "Vasco da Gama, a gentleman of your household, came to my country, whereat I was pleased. My country is rich in cinnamon, cloves, ginger, pepper, and precious stones. That which I ask of you in return is gold, silver, corals, and scarlet cloth."

The Portuguese left on August 29. By the time they reached Malindi, there were not enough healthy crewmen to man the three ships. Gama split his sailors among the *Berrio* and the *São Gabriel*, and destroyed the *São Rafael*. Then they sailed south for the Cape of Good Hope. Gama and his men sailed around the landmark on March 20, 1499.

The *Berrio* arrived in Portugal on July 10, setting off a wild celebration. Gama, however, stopped during the journey home when his brother Paulo died. He did not reach Portugal until September. When he did, he was praised throughout the country. The king granted him a title, "Admiral of the Indian Seas." He also gave him a house and a large **pension**. And to fulfill the vow he had taken when Gama had set out two years earlier, King Manoel ordered construction to begin on the magnificent church of São Jeronimo in Lisbon.

The Portuguese quickly prepared another voyage to the Indies. This time, the fleet was very large—13 ships and 1,200 men. The commander was Pedro Álvares Cabral. Gama wasn't going along, but he gave Cabral some navigation tips. Once again, Bartholmeu Dias was going along. This time he planned to travel all the way to India.

When Cabral set out, he took Gama's advice and sailed in a wide arc to the west. He went much farther west than Gama himself had—so far that his ships spotted land to the west. It was the coast of South America. Cabral stopped there briefly to claim the land (today known as Brazil) for Portugal, and sailed on to India.

This was not the only discovery for Cabral's fleet. When the ships rounded the Cape of Good Hope, they were separated by a storm. Several, including Bartholomeu Dias's ship, sank in the violent tempests. One of the other caravels landed on a large island off the coast of Africa. The ship's commander, Lourenço Marques, claimed the island for Portugal. He had become the first European to set foot on Madagascar.

The Arabs and Portuguese engaged in bitter fighting for control of the Indian Ocean. Here, Portuguese ships fire upon an Arab **dhow***, or ship, with triangular sails.*

When Cabral and his remaining ships reached Calicut, the Arab traders were unhappy. If the Portuguese established a direct trade route, there would be no profit for the Muslims. Several battles occurred, and a number of Cabral's sailors were killed. Nevertheless, the Portuguese established trading posts at Calicut and Cochin. When Cabral returned home in the summer of 1501, his ships were loaded with valuable spices.

Vasco da Gama himself commanded the next expedition in 1502. With 15 well-armed ships, he sailed to India and forced the local rulers to make trade agreements with the Portuguese. When he returned the next year, Gama retired to his home.

In the years that followed, the Portuguese trade empire grew. Vasco da Gama received a share of the profits of every trade voyage to India. This made him one of the richest men in Portugal.

Twenty-five years after his first voyage to India, Vasco da Gama returned again. King Manoel had died in 1521, and the new king, João III, had heard about problems at the Portuguese colony at Cochin. He asked Gama to take over the colony, appointing him *viceroy* in 1524. Gama did as the king asked, but he did not live long enough to make many changes. He died on December 24, 1524. His body was brought back to Portugal and buried in a marble tomb in the church of São Jeronimo in Lisbon.

The voyages of the Portuguese explorers of the 1400s and 1500s helped establish Portugal as a world power. The Portuguese trade empire soon included China, Japan, the Spice Islands, and the Philippines. However, Portugal was too small to maintain and defend a worldwide network of trade

The beautiful church of São Jeronimo contains the tomb of Vasco da Gama, one of Portugal's greatest heroes.

outposts. By the start of the 18th century, the nation had lost its position as a world trade power to countries like England, Spain, the Netherlands, and France. Despite this, the Portuguese influence on the cultures of Africa, Brazil, and the lands of the Indian Ocean remains even to this day.

The voyage of Vasco da Gama was built upon the discoveries of hundreds of brave sailors who came before him. It forced contact between the cultures of Europe and Asia, and inspired other countries to begin seeking new lands and establishing colonies over the next several centuries.

Chronology

1179 King Afonso I establishes the kingdom of Portugal.

1341 Three ships sent by King Afonso IV visit the Canary Islands.

1394 Prince Henry the Navigator is born.

1414 The successful Portuguese invasion of the Moslem stronghold at Ceuta inspires Prince Henry to look into nautical exploration.

1420 Portuguese expeditions sent by Prince Henry discover the Madeira Islands.

1420s Gonçalo Velho Cabral discovers the Azores Islands.

1434 Gil Eanes sails past Cape Bojador.

1441 Nuno Tristão reaches Cape Blanc; Antão Gonçalves brings the first black slaves from Africa to Portugal.

1444 Dinís Dias reaches Cape Verde, the westernmost point of Africa.

1457 Alvise da Cadamosto discovers the Cape Verde Islands.

1460 Prince Henry the Navigator dies.

1469 King Afonso V leases exploration rights along the African coast to Fernão Gomes. Over the next five years, Gomes's explorers extend Portugal's knowledge of the coast 2,000 miles southward.

1482 Diogo Cão reaches the mouth of the Congo River.

1487 Pero da Covilhã and Afonso de Paiva are sent by King João II to cross Africa and find India; Bartolomeu Dias sets off with three ships to sail around Africa to India.

1488 Dias rounds Cape of Good Hope and returns to Portugal.

1491 King João receives information from Covilhã and begins planning an expedition around Africa.

1493 Christopher Columbus returns to Spain, announcing that he has discovered a westward route to the Indies. Columbus does not realize he has instead found the New World.

1494 Pope Alexander VI issues the Treaty of Tordesillas, dividing newly discovered lands between Spain and Portugal.

1497 Vasco da Gama sets out with four ships for India. After stopping at several ports on the east coast of Africa, he reaches the city of Calicut on the west coast of India. In 1499, Gama returns to Portugal in triumph.

1500 En route to India, Pedro Alvares Cabral discovers Brazil and claims it for Portugal; Bartolomeu Dias's ship sinks in a storm off the Cape of Good Hope; the island of Madagascar is discovered by Lourenço Marques.

1502 Gama makes his second voyage to India with 15 well-armed warships and forces local rulers into trade agreements.

1524 Vasco da Gama becomes viceroy of India; dies at Cochin on December 24.

Glossary

banish–to exile a person, or drive that person away from his or her home.

bombard–a type of cannon used on Portuguese warships.

cape–a point of land that projects into the sea.

caravan–a company of travelers on a journey through desert or hostile regions. People traveled in caravans to protect themselves from bandits and brigands.

caravel–a sturdy sailing ship developed by the Portuguese in the 15th century. A caravel had a broad hull, a high and narrow deck at the at the back, and usually three masts.

civil war–a war between citizens of the same country.

crusades–military expeditions undertaken by Christian countries against the Muslims who lived in the Holy Land.

dhow–an Arab sailing ship with triangular sails (this is called "lateen rigging").

equator–an imaginary east-west line that divides the earth into two equal parts, the Northern and Southern hemispheres.

flagship–a ship that carries the commander of a fleet.

geography–the study of the earth's form, and its division into land and sea areas.

hemisphere–half of the earth.

Moors–Arabs from North Africa who invaded the Iberian Peninsula in the eighth century. Because the Moors followed Islam, they were involved in a series of bloody wars with the Christian people of Portugal and Spain.

Muslims–people who follow the Islamic religion.

navigation–the science of directing the course of a seagoing vessel, and of determining its position.

padrão–a large stone monument carved with the crest of Portugal; used to claim new lands for the king of Portugal.

pension–a fixed amount of money that is paid regularly to a person. A country's ruler or government may grant a pension to someone who deserves a reward for service.

pilot–a skilled sailor who is qualified to take charge of a ship entering or leaving a local harbor.

regent–the person who governs a kingdom if the rightful ruler is too young, absent, or unable to rule.

scurvy–a disease caused by lack of vitamin C, which was common on long sea voyages. Its signs include spongy gums and loose teeth, soreness in the arm and leg joints, and bleeding into the skin and mucous membranes.

spices–any of various aromatic vegetable products, such as pepper or nutmeg, used to season or flavor foods. In the 15th and 16th centuries, spices were rare and highly valued by the people of Europe.

storeship–a large ship that carried extra food and water to resupply other ships during long sea voyages.

sultan–a title referring to the ruler of a Muslim city or country.

viceroy–the governor of a country, who rules as the representative of a king.

Further Reading

Cuyvers, Luc. *Into the Rising Sun: Vasco da Gama and the Search for the Sea Route to the East.* New York: TV Books, 1999.

Fritz, Jean. *Around the World in a Hundred Years: From Henry the Navigator to Magellan.* Illustrated by Anthony Bacon Venti. New York: Putnam Publishing Group, 1994.

Mason, Antony, and Keith Lye. *The Children's Atlas of Exploration: Follow in the Footsteps of the Great Explorers.* Brookfield, CT: Millbrook Press, 1993.

Stefoff, Rebecca. *Vasco da Gama and the Portuguese Explorers.* New York: Chelsea House Publishers, 1993.

Subrahmanyam, Sanjay. *The Career and Legend of Vasco da Gama.* New York: Cambridge University Press, 1998.

Index

Afonso I (King of Portugal), 12
Afonso II (King of Portugal), 22, 24,
    27, 28
Africa, 8, 12, 17, 18, 19, 21, 23, 24, 25,
    26, 27, 28, 29, 31, 34-35, 36, 38,
    39, 41, 42, 45, 46, 47, 49, 54, 57
Asia, 8, 9, 13, 14, 18, 38, 42

Baldaia, Afonso, 21, 22
Barros, João de, 39
Berrio, 44, 46, 51, 53
Brazil, 54, 57

Cabral, Pedro Álvares, 54, 55
Cadamosto, Alvise, 25
Calicut, 51, 52, 53, 55
Canary Islands, 18, 24, 44
Cão, Diogo, 29, 31, 32, 33, 34, 35, 36
Cape Blanc, 23, 26
Cape Bojador, 19, 21
Cape Cross, 36, 37
Cape of Good Hope, 39, 41, 49, 50,
    53, 54
Cape Palma, 28
Cape St. Catherine, 31
Cape St. Mary, 34, 36
Cape Verde, 26, 27, 28
Cape Verde Islands, 27, 45, 46
Ceuta, 15, 16, 17
Cochin, 55, 56
Coelho, Nicolão, 44
Columbus, Christopher, 42, 43, 47
Congo River, 32, 33, 34, 35
Covilhã, Pero da, 36, 41, 42

Dias, Bartolomeu, 8, 36, 37, 38, 39, 44,
    46, 50, 54
Duarte I (King of Portugal),

Eanes, Gil, 19, 21

Gama, Paulo de, 44, 53

Gama, Vasco da, 8, 9, 43, 44, 46, 47,
    49, 50, 51, 52, 53, 54, 56, 57
Gomes, Diogo, 27
Gomes, Fernão
Gonçalves, Antão, 23
Gonçalves, Lopo, 28
Guinea, 17, 18, 27

India, 8, 14, 36, 38, 44, 51, 54, 56
Indian Ocean, 38, 42, 50, 57

João I (king of Portugal), 15
João II (king of Portugal), 29, 33, 34,
    35, 36, 39, 41, 42, 43
João III (king of Portugal), 56

Lisbon, 7, 9, 27, 31, 34-36, 39, 44, 54

Madeira Islands, 18
Madagascar, 54
Malindi, 51, 53
Manoel I (King of Portugal), 7, 9, 43,
    44, 53, 56
Moçambique, 50-51

Paiva, Afonso de, 36, 41
Pedro (Regent of Portugal), 22-23, 24
Pó, Fernando, 28
Polo, Marco, 12-13
Portugal, 7, 9, 11, 12, 14, 15, 17, 19, 22,
    24, 27, 29, 36, 42, 43, 53, 54, 56-
    57
Prince Henry the Navigator, 14-19, 21,
    22, 24, 25, 26, 27, 28, 29, 43, 51

Sagres, 18, 19
São Gabriel, 8, 44, 53
São Rafael, 8, 9, 44, 46, 53
South America, 47, 54
Spain, 11, 42, 43

Tristão, Nuno, 23-24

Picture Credits

JIM GALLAGHER is the author of more than 10 books for young adults, including biographies of Ferdinand Magellan and Hernando de Soto in the Chelsea House series EXPLORERS OF NEW WORLDS. A former newspaper editor and publisher, he lives near Philadelphia.